Habitat Days and

DAY AND NIG

Savannah

by Mary Boone

raintree
a Capstone company — publishers for children

Raintree is an imprint of Capstone Global Library Limited, a company incorporated in England and Wales having its registered office at 264 Banbury Road, Oxford, OX2 7DY – Registered company number: 6695582

www.raintree.co.uk
myorders@raintree.co.uk

Hardback edition © Capstone Global Library Limited 2023
Paperback edition © Capstone Global Library Limited 2024
The moral rights of the proprietor have been asserted.

All rights reserved. No part of this publication may be reproduced in any form or by any means (including photocopying or storing it in any medium by electronic means and whether or not transiently or incidentally to some other use of this publication) without the written permission of the copyright owner, except in accordance with the provisions of the Copyright, Designs and Patents Act 1988 or under the terms of a licence issued by the Copyright Licensing Agency, 5th Floor, Shackleton House, 4 Battle Bridge Lane, London SE1 2HX (www.cla.co.uk). Applications for the copyright owner's written permission should be addressed to the publisher.

Edited by Jessica Rusick
Designed by Hilary Wacholz
Original illustrations © Capstone Global Library Limited 2023
Picture research by Kelly Doudna
Originated by Capstone Global Library Ltd
Printed and bound in India

978 1 3982 4188 6 (hardback)
978 1 3982 4189 3 (paperback)

British Library Cataloguing in Publication Data
A full catalogue record for this book is available from the British Library.

Acknowledgements
We would like to thank the following for permission to reproduce photographs: iStockphoto: 1001slide, Cover (savanna), 1, 25ehaag6, Cover (giraffe), 1; Mighty Media, Inc.: 20, 21; Shutterstock: Benjamin B, 17, Dave Montreuil, 9, EcoPrint, 15, kavram, 18, Kelsey Green, 19, Kobus Peche, 16, Linda Marie Caldwell, 13, Pavel Krasensky, 12, Pearl Media, 14, PHOTOCREO Michal Bednarek, 5, Stu Porter, 11, thoron, 8, tonyzhao120, 7

Every effort has been made to contact copyright holders of material reproduced in this book. Any omissions will be rectified in subsequent printings if notice is given to the publisher.

All the internet addresses (URLs) given in this book were valid at the time of going to press. However, due to the dynamic nature of the internet, some addresses may have changed, or sites may have changed or ceased to exist since publication. While the author and publisher regret any inconvenience this may cause readers, no responsibility for any such changes can be accepted by either the author or the publisher.

Contents

What are savannahs?............................4

Morning 6

Midday..8

Late afternoon 10

Evening... 12

Night... 14

Late night 16

Dawn 18

    Giraffe activity 20

    Glossary 22

    Find out more 23

    Index 24

    About the author......................... 24

Words in **bold** are in the glossary.

What are savannahs?

Savannahs are grassy **habitats**. They have scattered **shrubs** and trees. Savannahs are hot during the day. They cool down at night.

Savannahs are found in Africa, South America, Asia and Australia. They are home to many animals. Some come out during the day. Others come out at night.

An African savannah

Morning

The sun rises over an African savannah. A giraffe eats while it is still cool. It plucks leaves from the tops of trees. Its long neck and tongue help it to reach.

Giraffes are the world's tallest **mammals**. They spend much of their time eating. Some giraffes eat 34 kilograms (75 pounds) of food each day.

Giraffe

Midday

The midday sun is hot. A thirsty elephant circles a baobab tree. Baobab trees have water in their trunks. The elephant scrapes off the tree's bark with its **tusks**. Then it makes a hole in the tree. The elephant reaches inside to get the water.

Baobab tree

Elephant

Late afternoon

A cheetah chases a gazelle. The big cat can run up to 113 kilometres (70 miles) per hour! The cheetah knocks the gazelle down. It bites the animal with its teeth.

Many big cats hunt at night. But cheetahs can't see well in the dark. They hunt during the day. Cheetahs also hunt in daylight to avoid other **predators**.

A cheetah chasing a gazelle

Evening

A termite mound towers over the savannah. Termites built the mound from soil, spit and poo. Some mounds are more than 9 metres (30 feet) tall!

Termites

A leopard on a termite mound

Termites live in a nest below the mound.
At sunset, they prepare to leave the nest.
They will gather wood to eat.

Night

The air cools. A cape porcupine sniffs for food. It finds an animal bone. The porcupine carries the bone to its **burrow**. It chews the bone to get **minerals**.

Cape porcupine

Springhare

A springhare digs for roots and seeds. Its large eyes help it to see in the dark. The springhare hears a noise. It leaps away using its strong back legs.

Late night

Shrieks and whoops **echo** across the savannah. A hyena clan is on the move. Hyenas sometimes eat animals killed by other predators. They also hunt.

The clan spots a gemsbok separated from its herd. The hyenas chase the gemsbok. They take the animal down together.

Gemsbok

Hyena

Dawn

The sun rises. An aardvark has spent the night searching for ants and termites. Now it returns to rest in its burrow.

Other animals wake. Kingfishers whistle and chirp. Zebras eat grass. Another day on the savannah has begun.

Aardvark

Giraffe activity

What you need:

- yellow paper
- cardboard tube
- glue stick
- brown paper
- pencil
- scissors
- black felt-tip pen

What to do:

1. Wrap a sheet of yellow paper around a cardboard tube. Glue the seam.

2. Tear a sheet of brown paper into small pieces. These are the giraffe's spots.

3. Glue the spots onto the cardboard tube. This is the giraffe's neck.

4. Draw an oval on yellow paper. Add ears and two small horns to the oval. This is the giraffe's head.

5. Cut out the giraffe's head.

6. Draw eyes and nostrils on the head with a black felt-tip.

7. Glue the head to one end of the cardboard tube. Put on a puppet show with your giraffe!

Glossary

burrow tunnel or hole in the ground made or used by an animal

echo repeat over and over again

habitat natural place and conditions in which a plant or animal lives

mammal warm-blooded animal that breathes air; mammals have hair or fur; female mammals feed milk to their young

mineral natural chemical that animals need to stay healthy

predator animal that hunts other animals for food

shrub plant or bush with woody stems that branch out near the ground

tusk long, pointed tooth that sticks out when an animal's mouth is closed

Find out more

Books

African Savannah, Claire Llewellyn (Kingfisher, 2015)

Animals (DKfindout!), DK (DK Children, 2016)

Habitats (Map Your Planet), Rachel Minay (Franklin Watts, 2021)

Websites

www.bbc.co.uk/bitesize/topics/zx882hv
Learn more about habitats and the environment.

www.dkfindout.com/uk/animals-and-nature/habitats-and-ecosystems
Find out more about animal habitats around the world.

Index

aardvarks 18
Africa 4, 6

baobab trees 8

cape porcupines 14
cheetahs 10

elephants 8

gazelles 10
gemsbok 16

giraffes 6
grasses 4, 18

hyenas 16

kingfishers 18

springhares 15

termites 12, 13, 18

zebras 18

About the author

Mary Boone has written more than 60 non-fiction books for young readers, ranging from biographies to craft guides. Mary lives in Washington, USA, where she shares an office with an Airedale Terrier called Ruthie Bader.